Children's Museum

Julie Murray

Abdo Kids Junior
is an Imprint of Abdo Kids
abdobooks.com

Abdo

FIELD TRIPS

Kids

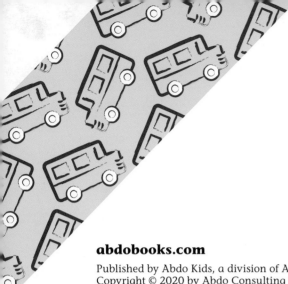

abdobooks.com

Published by Abdo Kids, a division of ABDO, P.O. Box 398166, Minneapolis, Minnesota 55439.
Copyright © 2020 by Abdo Consulting Group, Inc. International copyrights reserved in all countries.
No part of this book may be reproduced in any form without written permission from the publisher.
Abdo Kids Junior™ is a trademark and logo of Abdo Kids.

Printed in the United States of America, North Mankato, Minnesota.

102019
012020

THIS BOOK CONTAINS
RECYCLED MATERIALS

Photo Credits: Getty Images, iStock, Media Bakery, Shutterstock, ©Bob Linsdell p.11 / CC BY 2.0,
©User:mliu92 p.22 / CC BY-SA 2.0

Production Contributors: Teddy Borth, Jennie Forsberg, Grace Hansen

Design Contributors: Christina Doffing, Candice Keimig, Dorothy Toth

Library of Congress Control Number: 2019941203
Publisher's Cataloging-in-Publication Data

Names: Murray, Julie, author.
Title: Children's museum / by Julie Murray
Description: Minneapolis, Minnesota : Abdo Kids, 2020 | Series: Field trips | Includes online
    resources and index.
Identifiers: ISBN 9781532188732 (lib. bdg.) | ISBN 9781532189227 (ebook) | ISBN 9781098200206
    (Read-to-Me ebook)
Subjects: LCSH: Children's museums--Juvenile literature. | Museums--Juvenile literature. | Interactive art--
    Juvenile literature. | School field trips--Juvenile literature.
Classification: DDC 371.384--dc23

Table of Contents

Children's Museum

It's field trip day! The class is going to the children's museum.

It is a place where kids can play. They can explore. They can learn.

6

Kay plays with blocks.

She builds a tower.

8

Sam pours the water.

She watches it spin.

Lea makes a big bubble.

It pops!

Ray uses the paint.

He paints a tree.

14

Sue looks at a leaf. She uses a **microscope**.

Lain plays in the store.

He shops for groceries.

Have you been to a

children's museum?

Children's Museum Activities

building

painting

playing store

water fun

Glossary

explore

to move through in order to learn.

museum

a building in which objects of interest are stored and shown.

microscope

an instrument that uses a lens to make very small objects larger so they can be seen by the eye.

Index

Abdo Kids
ONLINE
FREE! ONLINE MULTIMEDIA RESOURCES

Visit **abdokids.com**
to access crafts, games,
videos, and more!

Use Abdo Kids code
FMK8732
or scan this QR code!